M.

CAPITAL PUNISHMENT

TROUBLED
SOCIETY

CAPITAL
PUNISHMENT

Scott Robert Hays

The Rourke Corporation, Inc.

The Rourke Corporation, Inc.
P.O. Box 3328, Vero Beach, FL 32964

Hays, Scott Robert, 1959-
    Capital punishment / by Scott Robert Hays
        p.cm. — (Troubled society)
    Summary: Discusses capital punishment, whether it is applied fairly to everyone, and whether it does any good.
    Includes bibliographical references.
    ISBN 0-86593-074-0
    1. Capital punishment—United States—Juvenile literature.
[1. Capital punishment.]   I. Title.   II. Series.
HV8699.U5H38 1990
364.6'6'0973—dc20   90-8733
                                                                        CIP
                                                                         AC

Series Editor: Gregory Lee
Editors: Elizabeth Sirimarco, Marguerite Aronowitz
Book design and production: The Creative Spark,
    Capistrano Beach, CA
Cover photograph: Lowell Georgia/Photo Researchers, Inc.

Capital   \ *adjective* \   To be sentenced to death as a penalty in the eyes of the law {a *capital* crime}. An execution {capital punishment.}

Contents

ONE

AN EDUCATION ON DEATH ROW

When a man is caught stealing another man's wallet, he is punished for his crime. The laws of our land set limits on his penalty. He may be fined or sentenced to jail. It is up to a judge or jury to decide.

When a man murders another man, he also is punished. But should society have the option of executing him as a form of punishment? Should the American legal system permit the killing of another human being?

Ever since the birth of this nation, Americans have argued about the death penalty. Does it obey the laws of the land? Does it discourage criminals from a life of crime? Is it a decent form of punishment?

To this day, Americans still do not agree on capital punishment. Those in favor of the death penalty see it as a just punishment for certain horrible crimes. Those opposed say it serves no useful purpose.

Capital punishment is a deadly serious issue. No one argues that society has the right to protect its citizens. One of the functions of government is to punish criminals who prey upon others. But to what extent?

Maryland's gas chamber. The condemned prisoner is strapped into the chair and the chamber is sealed before lethal cyanide gas is released, suffocating the inmate within minutes.

Could you sentence a person to die for killing another? What if it were your brother who was killed? Someday you may be asked to make this life or death decision while sitting on a jury.

Thirty-six states and the United States armed forces have death penalty laws. Yet executions are seldom carried out.

Since July 2, 1976, 121 people have been executed in the United States. Nearly all executions have taken place

in the South: Alabama, Florida, Georgia, Louisiana, Mississippi, North Carolina and Virginia.

Capital Crimes

Murder is not the only crime for which a person can receive a sentence of death. Treason and kidnapping are just two of the more common crimes that fall under capital punishment laws. But most of the executions within the last 14 years have been for felony murders. Felony murders include killing for hire; killing a police officer, judge or firefighter; and killing more than one person. Only one in 100 murderers is sentenced to die.

Many states have laws that make it easier to prosecute someone under capital punishment laws if a judge or jury finds the crime to be especially "cruel, horrible or brutal." As a result, those opposed to capital punishment are often forced to defend this country's worst criminals.

Crime tends to arouse the emotions. Violent crime, especially, makes us angry and full of rage. In turn, we seek justice. Charles Manson and Ted Bundy are examples of criminals who aroused the public's emotions.

Public opinion polls show that most citizens are in favor of capital punishment. Proponents will claim it discourages criminals from a life of crime, while opponents will argue that it is morally wrong to kill another human being, whatever the crime.

Although the Constitution guarantees every citizen a fair trial, a trial does not always result in an accurate verdict. The chance of executing innocent people is very real. And executing a murderer certainly will not

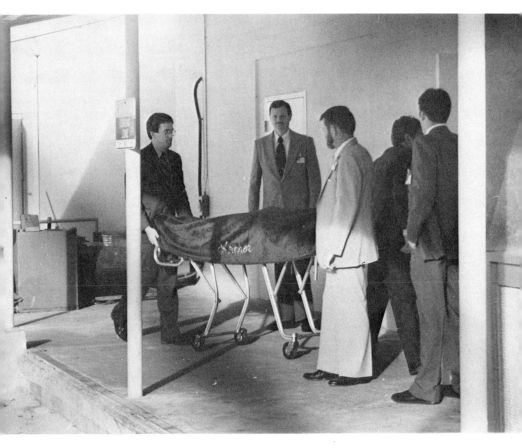

The body of Theodore "Ted" Bundy arrives at the Gainesville, Florida, medical examiner's office after his execution. Bundy was convicted of three murders, but as his appeals were exhausted he confessed to many more unsolved murders.

bring the victim back to life.

One alternative to the death penalty is life in prison. Unfortunately, criminals are often set free on parole. Can murderers be released without worrying that they will prey upon the public again?

The American jury plays an important role in sending men and women to their deaths. In all but a handful of states that have capital punishment laws, the jury alone is responsible for handing down the death

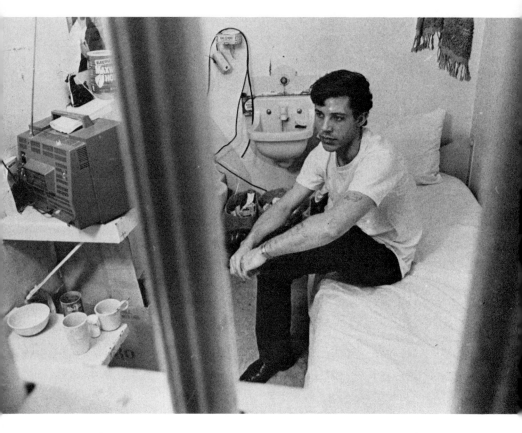

Terry Selman, age 25, is allowed a personal television set in his Louisiana State Prison cell. Except for one hour of exercises each day, Selman is confined to this small room while he awaits execution.

sentence. This places the state's power to execute a convicted criminal in the hands of a group of its citizens which helps limit state power.

Thirty states with capital punishment laws give the jury the responsibility of awarding the death penalty. In three other states, the jury decides whether the verdict is life or death, but the judge has the power to reverse the decision.

More than 2,100 prisoners (including more than 270 in California) are now waiting on *death row,* the nickname for the cellblocks where condemned prisoners are held. Their sentences are in various stages of appeal. It is important that death penalty cases move slowly through the legal system, as the process of appeal helps avoid errors.

Knowledge about the death penalty is good for everyone. The more you know, the better able you are to make an "informed" decision about the legal and moral points of this law.

TWO

Eye For Eye, Tooth For Tooth

The issue of capital punishment dates back to a time when people first lived together in a community. Government was formed to help protect citizens. Laws were written to help decide crime and punishment.

In ancient history, criminals were brought to an arena to be killed in public games. Other penalties for serious crimes included being nailed to a cross, hanging and beheading. During the Middle Ages, "witches" were stoned or burned to death.

As far back as 1792, a Philadelphia physician took it upon himself to call for an end to capital punishment. He argued that a sentence of life in prison allowed a criminal the chance to change himself for the better.

Those in favor of the death penalty argue that if, for example, "A" murders "B," then A should pay for B's life with his own. The execution of A will make sure that he does not kill again, and it will deter others from following his example. These are still the basic points used in today's debate on capital punishment.

The shaping of capital punishment laws evolved over time. They have gone through many changes, most notably in the last 30 years. In 1967, for example, the United States Supreme Court decided that the use of capital punishment was not in keeping with the spirit of the Constitution. For almost a decade the death penalty was not used in this country.

Then, in 1976, the high court ruled again in favor of some applications of the death penalty if the states wanted it. This time the court gave vague guidelines for jurors and upheld laws that left room for mercy. It also explained that

Charles Manson—America's most notorious prisoner—
was convicted in Los Angeles of conspiracy and murder charges.
Manson is serving a life term in California, although
public opinion in the state is clearly in favor of the death penalty
for the type of crimes Manson and his co-defendants committed.

Executions from the Middle Ages. Beheading and hanging were the most common, and were frequently held in public as an example to others. Unfortunately, executions were viewed by many people as entertaining.

The Execution of a Criminal.—From a Saxon MS.

use of the death penalty might be in violation of the federal law against "cruel and unusual punishment."

Six months later, the first execution under the "new" death penalty laws took place: Gary Gilmore was shot by a firing squad in Utah for murder.

Today, the process from conviction to execution is a long and winding road. However, the legal system is set up in a way to help judges and juries avoid making mistakes.

When a defendant goes on trial for his or her life, a jury or judge will have at least one, and usually two, things to determine. First, it must decide whether the defendant is guilty. Second, if the defendant is found guilty, a fitting punishment must be imposed. Under many of the new death penalty laws, a fitting punishment would either be life imprisonment or death.

Many state and federal law enforcement officials want to make it a capital crime—without exception—when a police officer is killed by a criminal. These two New York City policemen died in the line of duty.

One of the most crucial issues in deciding on a penalty is the question of *insanity*. Insanity is a legal term used to describe someone who is mentally ill or who did not understand what he or she was doing at the time of their crime.

Insanity is a legal defense in every state. If a defendant can satisfy the jury that his crime was the result of insanity, he may be given life in a mental hospital instead of the death penalty.

Once a defendant is convicted, a second hearing is held. During this hearing, the jury (or judge) decides between life and death. When a defendant is sentenced to death, his case is almost always appealed to a higher

The Long
and Winding Road

In most states, death sentences are always appealed. Here is a partial list of the legal steps available to a defendant through the American legal system after death penalty conviction:

- State Supreme Court appoints an attorney for the defense.
- Defense reviews the record.
- Defense files a brief asking the state Supreme Court for a new trial. They also request that the death verdict be overturned.
- State attorney general responds to defense brief.
- The state Supreme Court hears arguments. If the death penalty is upheld, defense will file for a rehearing.
- Defense appeals to U.S. Supreme Court. If request is denied, defense files another appeal that claims the federal court made a mistake.
- Once all appeals have been used up, the case goes before the governor for a clemency hearing.
- If clemency is denied, defense tries to appeal to any court that will listen.

court. Most appeals have to do with law, not fact. After the appeals, the defendant has the last option of *clemency*. Clemency means changing a sentence of death to one of life imprisonment.

For federal crimes, the power to reduce a death sentence belongs solely to the president of the United States. In states, the power is usually in the governor's hands. Some governors who oppose capital punishment may reduce all death sentences to life. Others consider it their duty to uphold the verdict and the state's law.

The 'D' Factor —Deterrence

No one yet has proved or disproved the theory that the threat of death discourages criminals from a life of crime. Clearly, both sides of the capital punishment issue disagree. It is an age-old argument. The *deterrence* premise is simple: If you hang a horse thief, it will discourage others from stealing horses.

In theory it sounds clear-cut, but does it work? America has more violent crimes today than ever before (the U.S. population is at its highest ever, as well). Some argue that the only reason we still have the death penalty is to satisfy people's itch for revenge. The only point that both sides can agree on is that the death penalty stops the convicted murderer from ever killing again. Some say this is reason enough to keep the death penalty.

What if the death penalty discouraged just one criminal from committing another criminal act? Is that a good enough reason to keep the death penalty? The problem with this argument is that it is hard to prove a crime did *not* happen. But if it did prevent just one murder, would it be worth it?

The U.S. Supreme Court—the last resort of many condemned murderers.
The Court has refused to overturn many death penalty convictions,
but has granted stays in some cases in order for appellate courts to
re-examine trial evidence before an execution is carried out.

The existence of the death penalty raises many such intriguing questions: If society truly believes that the death penalty deters criminals, why did it ban executions from public view in the 19th century? Why do we keep executions off television? Would it not help discourage others from a life of crime?

Some have argued that public executions would put an end to the death penalty, that we would find them barbaric. Are executions too brutal for society to watch? Is it better that we brush them under the rug where no one will see? Would you have second thoughts about sentencing a man to death if you had to watch him die?

These are questions that each citizen must consider.

Proponents of the death penalty argue that most would-be murderers are "not in their right mind" when they decide to kill another human being. To that end, most murderers do not think about the death penalty when they commit a crime. Still, many murders are *premeditated* (planned), and it is these murders to which proponents of the death penalty often point.

In 1976 the U.S. Supreme Court argued for *both* sides of the issue. In *Gregg v. Georgia*, the high court took the position that we may "assume safely that...the threat of death has little or no deterrent effect [on murderers] who act in passion." But for murders that were well thought out, "the death penalty is...a significant deterrent."

Here's another way to look at this issue. Does the threat of jail stop some of us from stealing another man's wallet? Wouldn't the threat of death also stop some of us from committing murder?

Capital punishment cannot and never will be

able to deter *all* murderers. But does this mean that it will not deter *any* murderers?

Opponents of the death penalty often argue that criminals can be rehabilitated, therefore executions are not needed. On the other hand, many murderers have been paroled and then killed again. Death puts an end to the possibility that a convicted murderer will commit further violent crimes. Execution is truly the last word.

Cruel and Unusual

Death penalty laws have long been attacked on the grounds that they violate the Constitution, the supreme law of our land. The U.S. Supreme Court interprets the Constitution, striking down any law or action it considers to be in conflict. Many men and women on death row have had their sentences set aside because of a decision by the high court. That is why death penalty laws have gone through many changes over the years.

In 1972, for example, the U.S. Supreme Court called for a temporary halt to executions because it violated the 8th Amendment to the Constitution. The decision came during a time when capital punishment had all but come to a stop. Then, in 1976, the high court made a ruling that began the process of allowing individual states to perform executions again.

Certain parts of the Constitution are used by defense attorneys to argue against the death penalty.

For example, some attorneys will argue that it is "cruel and unusual" punishment to sentence someone to death (the 8th Amendment prohibits "cruel and unusual" punishment). Others will argue that any attempt by the judicial system to deny a person his life is a violation of the 5th and 14th Amendments. By sentencing a man to death, society has denied him the right to clear his name and prove his innocence.

Ultimately, it is the nine U.S. Supreme Court justices who are forced to rule on these issues.

And Justice for All

In the past 50 years, more than half of all people executed in this country have been black. Yet the African-American community makes up only 12 percent of the population. One of the arguments against capital punishment is that any law that does not provide equal protection for all citizens is in violation of the 14th Amendment.

Of those awaiting execution on the nation's death rows, 42 percent are black. Some say this proves that blacks are treated unfairly when it comes to capital punishment cases. If that is true, argue the opponents, perhaps the death penalty should be thrown out of our justice system.

It cannot be denied that blacks, along with other ethnic groups, have been treated unfairly in this country. Among other wrongs done to African-Americans, they have often been denied basic civil rights. Naturally, we want the legal system to be fair. But is there enough clear evidence to suggest that racial discrimination exists where application of the death penalty is concerned?

A 1990 report by the U.S. General Accounting Office shows that discrimination persists. But statistics also show that violent crime—notably murder—is highest among the black community and other ethnic groups. Proponents of the death penalty argue that a high murder rate in one ethnic community means there will be an equally high rate of capital punishment cases in the same community.

Many legal challenges to the death penalty have been heard by the Supreme Court. Its most recent finding is that evidence of racial discrimination cannot, in and of itself, establish a violation of the Constitution. But if race is a factor in death penalty cases, what can and should be done to correct the injustice?

More and more blacks are now sitting in judgment of other blacks. We have more black judges and more black lawyers. And while the justice system may not always be just, it certainly sets up safeguards to prevent unjust acts. If racial discrimination exists in the legal system, it is not an argument against capital punishment, but rather an argument against the legal system. For if bias exists, it exists on every level. And if it exists on every level, the solution is to fix the bias, not do away with the punishment.

A Life Or Death Decision

Despite a trial by one's peers and more than seven years of appeals, mistakes can and do happen. In every capital case, it is possible that an innocent person may be executed. Is the killing of a few innocent people a price we must pay for having the death penalty? Without the death penalty, some people argue, we would not have to pay any price.

In 1846, Michigan set aside capital punishment. The law took effect on March 1, 1847. A decade earlier, a man was hanged just across the Detroit River. A few years later, another man confessed to the crime. In 1989, a man was released after spending more than 12 years in a Texas prison for a murder that someone else had committed.

In all criminal trials, jurors are told to vote guilty only if they are certain "beyond a reasonable doubt" that the defendant committed the crime. This is not the same as *absolute* certainty. A 1987 study found that at least 350 innocent people had been sentenced to death in the 20th century. More than 20 of these were executed. According to one specialist on capital punishment, there have been almost 30 cases since 1972 in which someone was convicted and sentenced to death, only to be freed later after the state admitted it had made a mistake. The most common reason given for these mistakes was lying by witnesses.

Some people would rather see a 100 guilty persons go free than have one innocent person face execution, but the matter of capital punishment is much more complicated than that.

"All human activities—flying, driving, playing football—occasionally lead to the death of innocent people. We don't give up these activities because the advantages outweigh the disadvantages," argues Ernest van den Haag, retired professor of law at Fordham University. "So I am in favor of the death penalty because it protects society more than any other possible penalty could."

Proponents also say wrongful executions are possible, but unlikely. Every time a guilty person is convicted of murder but not sentenced to death and executed, that person may kill again. For others, if even one innocent person is executed, it is one too many.

The only thing we know for certain is that the right to life for all innocent citizens is beyond dispute.

THREE

LIFE ON DEATH ROW

If you agree with the concept of capital punishment, you must also accept the reality of death. Executions are not always quick and efficient.

In 1983, for example, a prisoner had convulsions for eight minutes as he was being gassed. It took another prisoner 14 minutes to die as he was being electrocuted. Three separate charges of electricity caused smoke and flame to erupt from his left temple.

The ritual of death has changed little over the years. Once a prisoner is brought to a holding cell, he is constantly watched until he is taken to the execution chamber, where a telephone line is kept open to the state's governor for any last-minute *reprieve* or reversal of the sentence.

The following people are just a few of this country's most infamous murderers. Three of the six—Caryl Chessman, Gary Gilmore and Ted Bundy—have been executed. The other three—Richard Ramirez, Randy Kraft and Robert Alton Harris—spend their days on death row, waiting to be executed.

Caryl Chessman used the legal system to fight his death sentence for nearly 12 years, beginning the modern era of seemingly endless appeals in capital cases. Chessman became a published author while in prison, steadfastly maintaining that he was innocent of kidnapping, robbery, and attempted rape.

Caryl Chessman

One of the most famous inmates to die at San Quentin, California, was Caryl Chessman. He became known as the "red light bandit." He was accused of flashing a red light into the eyes of couples parked in cars and rob-

bing them at gunpoint. On occasion, the "red light bandit" sexually assaulted his female victims.

Chessman never confessed to his crimes, claiming that he was innocent of even the sexual assault charges.

The jury found him guilty. He was convicted on 18 crimes, including attempted robbery, kidnapping for the purpose of rape, and attempted rape. He was sentenced to death.

Chessman lived in a tiny cell on death row at San Quentin state prison in California for 12 years. During that time, he smuggled out four books that became best-sellers. His execution took place on May 2, 1960. At one minute past 10:00 A.M., Chessman, age 39, walked into the gas chamber. Right up to the last moment, his lawyers scrambled to obtain a further *stay of execution* (delay).

Roughly 60 people were on hand to witness the execution. Chessman's wrists and legs were strapped to a chair. The chamber door was sealed and a bag of cyanide pellets was dropped into a bucket of acid. Gas filled the chamber. Within two minutes he was choking. Within six minutes he was dead.

Prior to his death, Chessman sent a letter to the media. It read, in part: "I...believe that before too many more years have passed we will realize the senseless tragedy...of capital punishment, and that we will have the courage and the vision to eliminate it."

Gary Gilmore

Gary Gilmore was the first person executed after the U.S. Supreme Court upheld a ruling in 1976 that found that the death penalty could be constitutional.

Gary Gilmore, the first man executed in the United States after the U.S. Supreme Court overturned its ruling that the death penalty was unconstitutional. Gilmore's life and death were explored at length in both print and film because of his case's notoriety in U.S. legal history. Gilmore was convicted of murdering a hotel clerk.

The legal route to execute him was a long and highly emotional one, and the struggle to end Gilmore's life received huge media attention.

Gilmore was convicted of killing a 25-year-old male motel clerk during a robbery in Utah. His mother pleaded for her son's life. On December 3, 1976, the U.S. Supreme Court temporarily blocked his execution. But 10 days later, the court cleared the way for his death. He died on January 17, 1977, when four bullets from a firing squad hit his chest. It took him two minutes to die.

Ted Bundy

Ted Bundy was convicted of the 1978 deaths of two college students and a 12-year-old Florida girl. He also had been charged with other murders on a college campus in Florida. He was tried, found guilty, and sentenced to die.

At the time of the murders, Bundy was a law student. He was first sentenced to death in 1979, but he spent years delaying his execution with legal tactics.

In the last few days before his death, he provided details in as many as 50 other murders in nine states. He was on death row for nearly 10 years. The night before his death, the U.S. Supreme Court voted three separate times against his pleas to stay alive.

On January 24, 1989, he died in Florida's electric chair. Shortly after he had died, a crowd of people outside the prison celebrated and set off fireworks. The scene was repeated as the white hearse carrying Bundy's body pulled away from the prison grounds.

Several mental health doctors said the celebration of Bundy's execution showed people's frustration with the country's failure to deal with the crime prob-

Ted Bundy, who was executed in January, 1989, was interviewed on the night before his death. In the nationally televised interview, Bundy gave his explanation for the horrible crimes he committed.

The Cost of
the Death Penalty

- A 1982 study put the cost of life imprisonment at about $600,000 per person.

- It cost taxpayers about *$1.8 million* for an
  execution.

- Another study by the University of California
  set a value of *$4.5 million* per execution.

Why do executions cost taxpayers more money than a sentence of life in prison? Because it takes anywhere from four to ten years for a convicted criminal to use up all his appeals. Capital cases require two trials: one for guilt or innocence, and one for sentencing.

As a result, many people feel we should not be using tax dollars to pay for the expense of carrying out the legal options of someone given the death penalty. Opponents of the death penalty would much rather have their dollars spent on other government tasks, such as job programs, drug rehabilitation, and improved law enforcement.

A system of justice, however, should not be based only on expense. For example, how much cost can we place on the lives and families of the victims of murderers?

Capital cases are at least three times more expensive to try than non-capital cases. As a taxpayer, how would you want your money spent? For appeals on capital punishment, or for other programs?

lem. Florida Governor Bob Martinez said that Bundy was one man "...that deserved the electric chair."

Richard (the "Night Stalker") Ramirez

Richard Ramirez was convicted of the "Night Stalker" slayings that haunted Southern California in 1985. As part of his crime spree, Ramirez had strangled, raped, shot and slashed the throats of his victims. He even poked out the eyes of one victim.

Superior Court Judge Michael Tynan said that Ramirez's actions displayed a cruelty "beyond any human understanding." The jury found him guilty of 13 murders and 30 other crimes. They urged that he die in the gas chamber.

Under California law, death sentences are always appealed. If Ramirez's appeals fail, he will be executed at San Quentin state prison, site of the state's gas chamber. His appeals are likely to take at least seven years.

Randy Kraft

Killer Randy Steven Kraft was sentenced to death in 1989. The 44-year-old computer consultant was convicted in the murders of 16 young men. Some believe his victims may have numbered more than 60. Most of the victims were dumped along freeway ramps or in remote areas. Many were sexually mutilated and tortured.

Superior Court Judge Donald A. McCartin said after the trial, "If anyone ever deserved the death penalty, he's got it coming." The evidence, say many who attended the trial, was overwhelming. Kraft, on the other hand, maintained his innocence. With automatic

Randy Kraft listens in a Santa Ana, California, courtroom as a jury recommends the death penalty for his two-decade murder spree.

appeals, it could take at least seven years before Kraft is executed.

Robert Alton Harris

For the first time in 23 years, California came within hours of executing a convicted murderer. To date, Robert Alton Harris has spent 11 years on death row. He also has gone through four appeals each by the California and U.S. Supreme Courts.

Harris was convicted of the 1978 killing of two

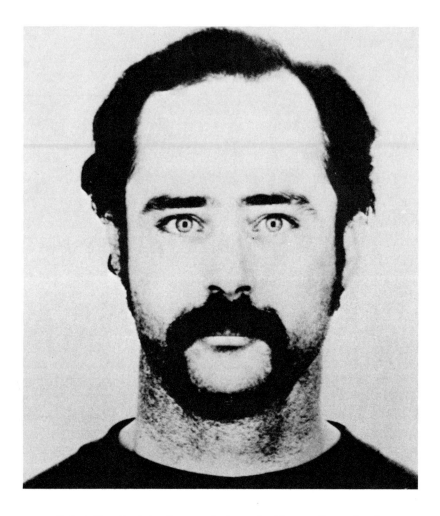

Robert Alton Harris has been on death row for 11 years. He murdered two teenage boys in 1978.

teenage boys he had kidnapped from a shopping center parking lot outside San Diego. He had wanted to use their car for a bank robbery, but instead he forced the two boys to drive him to a reservoir. Once there, he began shooting.

Harris confessed to the murders. He was sentenced to die in San Quentin's gas chamber. Five days before his execution, a federal appeals court judge blocked his execution. His attorneys argued that the murders he committed were the result of brain damage.

The state's attorney general asked the U.S. Supreme Court to lift the stay of execution and allow it to go forward as planned. The Court refused. In so doing, it spared Harris' life—at least for the time being. Harris will get a new hearing in federal court.

The basis of Harris' appeal has to do with the psychiatric evaluations that were given to him, and whether their conclusions were valid. The so-called "state of mind" of a convicted murderer is an important consideration in sentencing.

The father of one of the dead boys protested this latest appeal. He wanted to see Harris die. In fact, roughly 60 percent of California residents favored his execution, according to a poll taken by *The Los Angeles Times*. It was an important test for capital punishment foes. An execution in California, some believed, would have given other states the green light to start executing their death row inmates.

But what makes one serious crime so different from another, that an offender deserves to be sentenced to death instead of life in prison? California is not the only state that is finding it hard to decide which murderers should get life and which death.

FOUR

CRIME AND PUNISHMENT OF THE YOUNG

People under the age of 18 are legally considered juveniles. Juveniles who have committed murder and other crimes have not been spared from execution in the history of the United States.

When a juvenile commits a minor crime, the court can order either probation or sentence the youth to jail or a special facility for young offenders. When a juvenile murders another person, however, the court can use the full range of its sentencing powers, including a long term in prison or the death penalty. Should juveniles be executed?

Juveniles commit about nine percent of the homicides in the United States, according to one study. But how old does one have to be to be capable of conscious evil?

The first reported execution of a juvenile was in 1642 in Massachusetts. A 16-year-old was sentenced to death. Since then, of the approximate 15,000 executions carried out in the United States, roughly 280 were juvenile offenders who had committed their crimes before they were age 18. The last juvenile offender was executed on May 15, 1986, in Texas for a murder he committed at age 17.

Proponents of the juvenile death penalty argue that if a teenager has the capacity to murder another human being, he or she should be punished to the full extent of the law. Opponents argue that a juvenile's mental state is not fully developed, and that this fact alone should exempt him or her from the death penalty. Another argument is that if teenagers are too young to serve on juries, they should also be too young to be given the death penalty. By taking the position that teenagers are too young to make moral decisions, however, a court might rob them of some

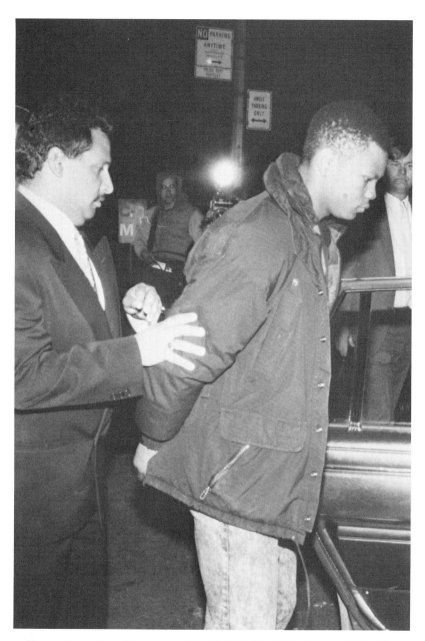

More and more juveniles are committing violent crimes. This 14-year-old boy, for example, was arrested on suspicion of rape. As convictions of juveniles grow for capital crimes, will more states execute minors for "adult" crimes?

of the freedoms they now enjoy.

Can juveniles be *rehabilitated*, that is, made to give up crime? Some argue that this should be the key element that bars them from the death penalty. Others go even further by stating that a civilized society simply should not execute offenders under the age of 18.

Many citizens support the death penalty because they believe it is legal revenge against the criminal. On this issue, it seems generally agreed that crimes committed by youths are just as harmful to victims as those committed by adults.

Does the youth of our society deserve less punishment because they may have less capacity to control their conduct and emotions?

Age, not mental maturity, is the sole basis by which our society determines when citizens can vote, drink alcoholic beverages, get married, buy a house, sign a contract, or serve in the military. To deny the offender under age 18 all of these rights and then impose the worst of adult punishments raises the question of justice.

Should society ignore the goals of reform for juvenile criminals? Many people can be rehabilitated, especially young adults.

Young And Restless

The year was 1982, when he was only 16 years old. It was the first time he had been on his own, and he was scared.

He had just been released from the custody of juvenile authorities, having been in and out of trouble since the age of 8. The first time was for trying to poison his mother's boyfriend. He claimed the man had beat

The Minimum Ages For Death

Here is a list of the 36 states that permit the death penalty and their minimum age laws:

Age	State
18	California, Colorado, Connecticut, Illinois, Nebraska, New Jersey, New Mexico, Ohio, Oregon, Tennessee
17	Georgia, New Hampshire, Texas
16	Nevada
15	Louisiana, Virginia
14	Alabama, Arkansas, Idaho, Kentucky, Missouri, North Carolina, Pennsylvania, Utah
13	Mississippi
12	Montana
10	Indiana
No Minimum	Arizona, Delaware, Florida, Maryland, Oklahoma, South Carolina, South Dakota, Washington, Wyoming

Georgia has carried out 41 death sentences of young adults, the most of any state. North Carolina and Ohio each have executed 19. As of 1988, only 33 people remained on death row for crimes committed while they were under the age of 18. Overall, 15 states are holding juveniles subject to the death penalty.

"Officer down"—the radio message that brings other police units in a hurry to the scene of an officer-involved shooting. The rookie police officer who was sitting in this patrol car was shot in the head.

him. Two years after that he was picked up for various petty crimes.

When he was older, he had dreams of joining the Air Force and learning to fly jets. But his dreams were shattered when he learned that the Air Force might not take him because of his criminal background. It was at that point that he quit dreaming. "I had no future," he told a reporter. "I'd been wrong, but by then the score was against me as a law-abiding citizen."

He tried to make it on his own, but he kept running into roadblocks. He was fired from a couple of jobs. So he lived at the foot of a cement statue in a park with his girlfriend. For food, he and a couple of other homeless teenagers would steal pizza or look in trash cans. They were always hungry.

He thought about buying a friend's motorcycle and traveling cross-country looking for the father he had not seen since the age of 5. But he needed money. So on July 27, 1985, he robbed a liquor store. During the robbery, he pulled out a knife and stabbed a 27-year-old mother of two to death. He was then just 19 years old.

He pleaded guilty to the 1985 murder and asked the judge to sentence him to death. "Death isn't a scary thing to someone who's hurting inside so bad they're hurting other people," he once said. "They're looking for death as a way out." On June 27, 1986, the judge granted him his wish. He spent his 20th birthday on death row, awaiting his fate.

The dead woman's husband wanted the young man to die. The memories of his wife's body with eight bloody stab wounds were still fresh in his mind after many years. The young murderer once told a doctor that he had nothing personal against the woman he had killed. He compared her to a trash can that he needed to kick out of his way.

His attorneys claimed he was abused as a young man. In fact, he had been sexually and physically abused by a boyfriend of his mother. At age five, an adult fed him drugs. "Everybody along the line washed their hands of him," said one of his attorneys.

During the first few weeks after his arrest he tried

The control panel to an electric chair. Note the timer—the lethal voltage is delivered in two and sometimes three jolts of different duration.

to hang himself. It wasn't until after he had arrived on death row that he started thinking about life rather than death.

He was asked what he would do if he were ever to go free. He said he would go to Australia, get a pilot's license, and ride away in an aircraft of his own design. He was then asked how he would react to life in prison, without the possibility of parole. "It [would] be like somebody discussing holding their hand in a flame for an hour. It's the first few seconds I'm worried about."

He is now age 24, still on death row, and still thinks the only way to pay for his crime is with his own life. Some people argue that this man deserves a chance to be rehabilitated because he has changed since he committed his crime.

The husband of the dead woman disagrees.

Some death penalty proponents argue that many "death row conversions" are merely show—a condemned murderer will admit their guilt and pretend to feel great remorse in order to earn a sentence of life rather than death.

FIVE

A VIEW FROM ABOVE

"And if *any* mischief follow, then thou shalt give life for life, Eye for eye, tooth for tooth..."
(Exodus 21: 23-24)

When all is said and done, most people base their opinions about capital punishment on moral grounds. It is really a personal decision: the death penalty is wrong, or the death penalty is just. When faced with a high murder rate in this country, which side would you choose?

Society teaches us that human life is to be valued and that to kill is wrong. Yet our society allows the death penalty to exist. By killing people who have killed, we do what the killers have done. We mirror the violence we seek to remove. But do we place a higher value on the life of a murderer than on the death of his or her victim?

Most moral arguments, of course, are not based on facts. Each is dealing on an emotional level. Most of the issues revolve around these three basic concerns:

1. Should society sanction the execution of any human life?
2. Does society have the right to punish antisocial behavior?
3. Is capital punishment cruel and unusual punishment?

These kinds of moral decisions for and against capital punishment carry a lot of weight with policymakers in our society, including the president of the United States and the justices of the U.S. Supreme Court. These are the people who help shape our laws about crime and punishment. They decide who should be punished and how. Are some punishments too cruel to be allowed into the legal system?

The morality of the death penalty is questioned by many people, including these protesters.

Are some criminals so hardened that no punishment is too severe?

A responsible society wants protection. Government would be worthless if it did not punish criminals who prey upon others. But what is due punishment?

In part, capital punishment is an expression of society's moral outrage at offensive conduct. For many, however, this is not a good enough reason to end a human life. But for others, capital punishment is essential in a society that asks its citizens to obey its laws, and allows the legal system to punish wrongdoers.

Moral arguments both for and against capital

STATE-BY-STATE

In all, 36 states and the United States armed forces have laws that permit capital punishment. Since 1976, the year the U.S. Supreme Court restored the death penalty, 13 states have executed a total of 121 people. Southern states have carried out all but 11 of those executions.

Executions

State	Since 1930	1976 to 1989
Alabama	138	7
Arizona	38	
Arkansas	118	
California	292	
Colorado	47	
Connecticut	21	
Delaware	12	
Florida	189	20
Georgia	379	14
Idaho	3	
Illinois	90	
Indiana	43	2
Iowa	18	
Kansas	15	
Kentucky	103	
Louisiana	151	18
Maryland	68	

Massachusetts	27	
Mississippi	157	4
Missouri	62	1
Montana	6	
Nebraska	31	
Nevada	31	4
New Hampshire	1	
New Jersey	74	
New Mexico	6	
New York	329	
North Carolina	266	3
Ohio	172	
Oklahoma	60	
Oregon	19	
Pennsylvania	152	
South Carolina	164	2
South Dakota	1	
Tennessee	93	
Texas	326	34
Utah	16	3
Vermont	4	
Virginia	99	8
West Virginia	40	
Washington	47	
Washington, D.C.	40	
Wyoming	7	

The following states have never had a death penalty conviction: Alaska, Hawaii, Maine, Michigan, Minnesota, North Dakota, Rhode Island and Wisconsin.

Methods of Execution

Alabama	Electrocution
Alaska	None
Arizona	Gas
Arkansas	Injection
California	Gas
Colorado	Injection
Connecticut	Electrocution
Delaware	Injection
Florida	Electrocution
Georgia	Electrocution
Hawaii	None
Idaho	Injection
Illinois	Injection
Indiana	Electrocution
Iowa	None
Kansas	None
Kentucky	Electrocution
Louisiana	Electrocution
Maine	None
Maryland	Gas
Massachusetts	None
Michigan	None
Minnesota	None
Mississippi	Injection
Missouri	Injection
Montana	Hanging, Injection

Nebraska	Electrocution
Nevada	Injection
New Hampshire	Injection
New Jersey	Injection
New Mexico	Injection
New York	None
North Carolina	Gas, Injection
North Dakota	None
Ohio	Electrocution
Oklahoma	Injection
Oregon	Injection
Pennsylvania	Electrocution
Rhode Island	None
South Carolina	Electrocution
South Dakota	Injection
Tennessee	Electrocution
Texas	Injection
Utah	Firing squad, Injection
Vermont	Electrocution
Virginia	Electrocution
Washington	Hanging, Injection
Washington, D.C.	None
West Virginia	None
Wisconsin	None
Wyoming	Injection
American Samoa, Guam, Puerto Rico,Virgin Is.	None

The Florida electric chair faces a gallery where witnesses view the execution behind a glass window. Witnesses are legally required to be present.

punishment have a lot going for them. That's why it is important—for both the proponents and opponents of capital punishment—that death penalty cases proceed slowly through the courts.

For the proponents, a lengthy review process

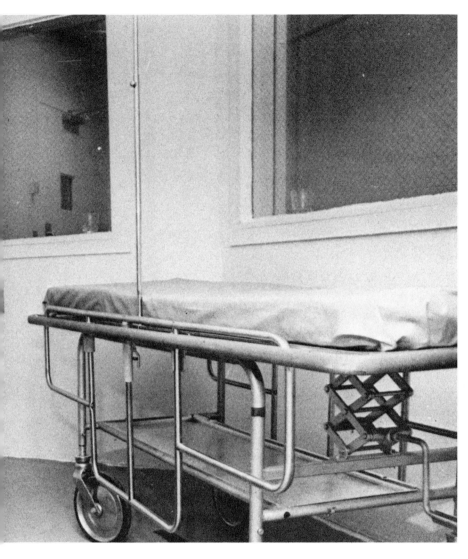

allows the system to work, and helps make sure that it is being managed fairly. For opponents, a lengthy review process keeps death row inmates alive and offers some hope that any errors commmitted in the process of conviction will be discovered and remedied before the tragedy of murder is compounded by the tragedy of a wrongful execution.

"[T]he simple fact is that the death penalty has been a gross failure. Beyond its horror...it has neither protected the innocent nor deterred the wicked."

—Edmund G. "Pat" Brown Sr.
former governor of California

"Crimes are committed not just against a victim, but against society. There must be...punishment for misbehavior. The punishment for [some] murder[s], not all murder[s], is death. The murderer has forfeited his right to live among us."

—Ernest van den Hagg
retired professor of law
Fordham University

GLOSSARY

APPEAL. A legal move by which a case is brought from a lower court to a higher court for rehearing.

CLEMENCY. An act that reduces the penalty for a crime.
CONVICT (verb). To find someone guilty of a crime.

DEATH ROW. A term used for the jail that houses criminals sentenced to death.
DETERRENCE. Discouraging a criminal act through fear of punishment.
DISCRIMINATION. The act or practice of favoring one person over another without cause, as in *racial discrimination*.
DUE PROCESS OF LAW. A course of action that guarantees a person fair treatment within established rules and laws.
EXECUTION. To put to death as a legal penalty.

FELONY MURDERS. Murder that falls under the laws of the federal government.

HOMICIDE. The killing of one human being by another.

IMPARTIAL JURY. A jury that is fair.
INSANITY. The state of being mentally ill or incompetant, making a person incapable of judging legal or illegal conduct.

JUVENILES. A young person under the age of 18.

OPPONENT. One who argues against a cause.

PAROLED. The release of a prisoner from jail under certain conditions.

PERJURY. To lie under oath in a court of law.

PROPONENT. One who argues in favor of a cause.

REHABILITATION. To restore a person to a condition of useful activity.

STAY OF EXECUTION. To stop an execution for a period of time.

TREASON. The offense of trying to overthrow government by use of force.

U.S. SUPREME COURT. The highest court of the United States. It has the power to hear all cases under U.S. law, including issues about the Constitution.

BIBLIOGRAPHY

"Back to Reason in Death Cases," *The Los Angeles Daily Journal* (editorial), Oct. 20, 1987: 4

Benau, Hugo Adam. "Death is Different: Studies in the Morality, Law, and Politics of Capital Punishment." Northeastern University Press, Boston, MA, 1987

Benau, Hugo Adam. "The Courts, the Constitution, and Capital Punishment." Lexington Books, Lexington, MA, 1977

Black, Charles L. Jr. "Capital Punishment: the Inevitability of Caprice and Mistakes." W.W. Norton & Company, New York, 1981

Brown, Edmund (Pat) and Dick Adler. "Public Justice, Private Mercy—A Governor's Education on Death Row." Weidenfeld & Nicolson, New York, c1989

Carrington, Frank G. "Neither Cruel Nor Unusual." Arlington House Publishers, New York, c1978

Gelman, David. "The Bundy Carnival: A Thirst for Revenge Provokes a Raucous Send-Off," *Newsweek*, Feb. 8, 1989, 66.

Greenhouse, Linda. "Court to Hear Challenge of Death

Penalty Law." *The New York Times*, March 28, 1989: A11(N)

Hass, Kenneth C. and James A. Inciardi. "Challenging Capital Punishment: Legal and Social Science Approaches." Sage Publications, Newbury Park, CA, 1988

Joyce, James Avery. "Capital Punishment: A World View." Grove Press, Inc., New York, c1961

Malcolm, Andrew H. "Tainted Trials Stir Fears of Wrongful Executions (Innocent persons released from death row heat up debate over controversy on death penalty)." *The New York Times*, May 3, 1989, A9(N)

Meltsner, Michael. "Cruel and Unusual: The Supreme Court and Capital Punishment." Random House, New York, 1973

Morain, Dan. "From Life of Horror to a Death Row Cell." *The Los Angeles Times*, April 2, 1990: 1

"New York Needs Life, Not Death." *The New York Times* (editorial), March 22, 1989: 14(N)

"No Room for Error: Mistakes Can and Do Occur with Prisoners Sentenced to Death." *The Los Angeles Daily Journal* (editorial), May 4, 1989: 6

Prejean, Helen. "And Several States are Discovering it also Costs Too Much to Carry Out." *The Los*

Angeles Daily Journal, Feb. 4, 1988: 4

"Race, Death, and Justice (Supreme Court decision on racially motivated distribution of death penalty)." *The Progressive* (editorial), June 1987: 8(2)

Rodricks, Dan. "The Clamor Over Delays Shows How the Death Penalty Cheapens Society." *The Los Angeles Daily Journal*, Feb. 4, 1988: 4

Roderick, Kevin. "Last Steps, Words on the Row." *The Los Angeles Times*, March 28, 1990: 1

Rohrlich, Ted. "Executions: Who Dies and Why?" *The Los Angeles Times*, April 2, 1990: 1

Rosenbaum, Ron. "Too Young to Die? (Wilkins and the juvenile death penalty)." *The New York Times Magazine*, March 12, 1989: 32

Sitomer, Curtis J. "Can We Kill Those Who May Not Understand?"*The Los Angeles Daily Journal* (from the *Christian Science Monitor*), Feb. 23, 1989: 6

Skelton, George. "Voters Favor Execution by Nearly 4 to 1." *The Los Angeles Times*, April 2, 1990: 1

"Why Execution is Dead Wrong." *The New York Times* (editorial), April 29, 1989: 14(N)

Index

Picture Credits